Dear Parent:

Congratulations! Your child is taking the first steps on an exciting journey. The destination? Independent reading!

STEP INTO READING® will help your child get there. The program offers five steps to reading success. Each step includes fun stories and colorful art. There are also Step into Reading Sticker Books, Step into Reading Math Readers, Step into Reading Write-In Readers, Step into Reading Phonics Readers, and Step into Reading Phonics First Steps! Boxed Sets—a complete literacy program with something for every child.

Learning to Read, Step by Step!

Ready to Read Preschool–Kindergarten
• big type and easy words • rhyme and rhythm • picture clues
For children who know the alphabet and are eager to begin reading.

Reading with Help Preschool–Grade 1
• basic vocabulary • short sentences • simple stories
For children who recognize familiar words and sound out new words with help.

Reading on Your Own Grades 1–3
• engaging characters • easy-to-follow plots • popular topics
For children who are ready to read on their own.

Reading Paragraphs Grades 2–3
• challenging vocabulary • short paragraphs • exciting stories
For newly independent readers who read simple sentences with confidence.

Ready for Chapters Grades 2–4
• chapters • longer paragraphs • full-color art
For children who want to take the plunge into chapter books but still like colorful pictures.

STEP INTO READING® is designed to give every child a successful reading experience. The grade levels are only guides. Children can progress through the steps at their own speed, developing confidence in their reading, no matter what their grade.

Remember, a lifetime love of reading starts with a single step!

For Chris, who still makes my heart race
—A.R.

Cover photograph: Photo by Elsa/Getty Images.
Interior photographs: Pages 3 and 42 (bottom): Photo by Elsa/Getty Images; pages 4–5: AP Photo/Paul Kizzle; page 6: AP Photo/David Graham; pages 8, 16 (bottom), 19, 21, 37, 44: Photos by RacingOne/Getty Images; pages 10 and 14: AP Photo; pages 12, 16 (top), 17: © Bettmann/CORBIS; page 22: Courtesy Ronald Reagan Library; page 23: George Bush Presidential Library and Museum; page 24: Courtesy of the Smithsonian Institution, NMAH/Transportation; pages 25 and 45: © George Tiedemann/GT Images/CORBIS; pages 27 and 32 (top): AP Photo/Terry Renna; page 29: © David Allio/Icon SMI/CORBIS; page 31: © Reuters/CORBIS; page 32 (bottom): Photo by Donald Miralle/Getty Images Sport; page 33: Photo by Tom G. Lynn/Time Life Pictures/Getty Images; pages 35 and 42 (top): AP Photo/Tom Russo; page 38: AP Photo/Roger Hart; page 39: AP Photo/Bebeto Matthews; page 40: AP Photo/Bob Jordan; page 41: © George Tiedemann/NewSport/CORBIS; page 46: AP Photo/MF; page 48: AP Photo/Bill Hudson.

Text copyright © 2009 by Angela Roberts

Published in the United States by Random House Children's Books, a division of Random House, Inc., New York.

Step into Reading, Random House, and the Random House colophon are registered trademarks of Random House, Inc.

Visit us on the Web! www.stepintoreading.com

Educators and librarians, for a variety of teaching tools, visit us at www.randomhouse.com/teachers

Library of Congress Cataloging-in-Publication Data
Roberts, Angela.
NASCAR's greatest drivers / by Angela Roberts. — 1st ed.
  p. cm. — (Step into reading. Step 5)
ISBN 978-0-375-84813-1 (pbk.) — ISBN 978-0-375-94813-8 (lib. bdg.)
[1. Automobile racing drivers—United States—Biography.
2. Stock car racing—United States—History.] I. Title.
GV1032.A1R6 2009
796.72092'2—dc22
[B] 2008002143

Printed in the United States of America 10 9 8 7 6 5 4 3 2 1 First Edition

NASCAR'S GREATEST DRIVERS

By Angela Roberts
With photographs

Random House 🏠 New York

Introduction
NASCAR Fever

Imagine zooming around a racetrack at nearly 200 miles per hour. It's over 120 degrees in your car. You're hot, thirsty, and strapped into a tiny seat. You must stay focused for 400, 500, even 600 miles as tens of thousands of roaring fans cheer you on. A lot of money is at stake. And pride. Will you be the first to cross the finish line?

There is no stopping a NASCAR driver—or the sport itself. There are NASCAR racetracks all over the country, from New York to California. Seventy-five million people call themselves NASCAR fans. The sport that started small on

dirt tracks and beaches in the South is now the hottest sport in America!

NASCAR is called *stock-car* racing because the cars driven in the early days of the sport came from a car dealer's regular supply, or *stock,* of cars. Today's stock-car racers still drive standard cars, although now they're made to be driven safely and quickly on a track. This makes NASCAR very different from other styles of racing. For example, Indy car racing has always used specially made race cars built from the ground up.

Unlike other sports with seasons of only a few months, NASCAR racing takes place almost all year long. The first race is in February. It's the big Daytona 500. The drivers have a chance to compete in thirty-five more races through November, racking up as many points as they can. They each hope to win the Nextel Cup, NASCAR's biggest prize! The champion claims the trophy and more than $5 million in bonus money.

Many NASCAR fans have a favorite driver. They love to wear hats and T-shirts to show their loyalty. There have been many great NASCAR stars for fans to cheer on. Let's meet some of the best of all time.

A sellout crowd watches as drivers take the green flag to start the Daytona 500.

Car #22 leads the way at the 1962 Daytona 500.

Glenn "Fireball" Roberts

(1929–1964)

February 18, 1962. Daytona Beach, Florida. A crowd of more than 58,000 fills the stands at one of NASCAR's newest and most important tracks, the Daytona International Speedway. Lots of them are there to root for the famous Fireball Roberts. He is one of NASCAR's most popular drivers, and his fans want to see him win!

Many great drivers are racing. But Fireball owns the road driving his #22 Pontiac. He takes the lead in 144 out of 200 laps. After three tough hours of racing, Fireball spots the checkered flag! He's close to the victory he wants so badly. Fireball presses the gas pedal and sails across the finish line only 27 seconds ahead of the second-place finisher. Fireball has done it! The crowd in Daytona Beach explodes in cheers. But Fireball is quiet. He's enjoying the victory he has dreamed about so many times.

■ ■ ■

Glenn Roberts grew up in Apopka, Florida, not far from Daytona Beach. It was there that he got the nickname Fireball, but it didn't come from car racing. It came from playing baseball. The name stuck. In 1945, when Glenn was in high school, his family moved to Daytona. Daytona was (and still is) one of the hot spots of car racing. There the racing bug bit Fireball hard.

In 1947, Fireball raced for the first time at a local race in North Wilkesboro, North Carolina. Three years later, he won his first official NASCAR race in Hillsborough, North Carolina. That year, he finished second in NASCAR in the number of points won. He was only twenty-one years old!

Fireball worked hard to learn all he could about racing and race cars. He wanted to be one of the very best. By 1957, Fireball had many

Fireball (left) poses after winning second place in the NASCAR Convertible stock-car race in Daytona Beach, February 25, 1956.

fans and many victories. That year, he was named NASCAR's Most Popular Driver.

Fireball had another big year in 1958. Of the ten races he entered that year, he won six, finished second in one, and was third in another. Fireball was the hero of a new era for NASCAR. Racetracks called superspeedways were being built. Superspeedways are at least one mile long and designed for top speeds. Fireball ruled these racetracks. He was named Florida's Professional Athlete of the Year. It was the first time the award was ever given to a race-car driver.

Soon Fireball began to talk about retiring from racing. He'd set over 400 records and was at the top of his sport. But he had other things he wanted to do. He wanted to fly his airplane and ride motorcycles. He decided to race just a few more times before leaving the track for good.

Sadly, he didn't make it to retirement. On

Fireball won the ninth annual Southern 500 stock-car race on August 1, 1958.

May 24, 1964, Fireball was driving in the World 600 race in Charlotte, North Carolina. Early in the race, he swerved to avoid a wreck and his car flipped. His fuel tank ripped open and exploded. Fireball was burned over 80 percent of his body. He spent six weeks in the hospital but never recovered. He was thirty-five years old. Fireball was buried in Daytona Beach, in a cemetery just behind the third turn at Daytona International Speedway. Fans and fellow drivers were heartbroken.

Two good things came from the death of Fireball Roberts. NASCAR quickly developed rubber fuel cells that are almost impossible to pierce. And racers started wearing fire-resistant uniforms. These safety features have saved many lives over the years. Because of this and his amazing career, Fireball Roberts will always be an important part of NASCAR.

Fireball (center) in 1960, four years before his untimely death.

Glenn "Fireball" Roberts

(1929–1964)

- Sometimes called the best NASCAR driver to never win the championship
- Thirty-three wins out of 206 races; in the top five 93 times, in the top ten 122 times
- Set over 400 records
- Won 1962 Daytona 500
- Named one of NASCAR's 50 Greatest Drivers
- International Motorsports Hall of Fame
- Motorsports Hall of Fame in America

Richard Petty

(b. 1937)

August 17, 1967. Columbia, South Carolina. Almost 7,000 fans stand around the dusty dirt track watching the Sandlapper 200 race. There are 199 laps down and one to go. All the drivers want to win, but the stakes are especially high for Richard Petty, in car #43.

Today's race has been wild. Out of twenty-four starters, twelve have left the track because of crashes or car trouble. If Richard can hang on and finish first, he'll have won the most races in any one season in NASCAR's history.

Richard in a cowboy hat (naturally!) in 1969.

Richard's 1967 Plymouth speeds around the last lap. He's able to stay in the lead! The crowd erupts as he flies through the checkered flags. Richard has just made history!

Even more amazing, he'll go on to win eight more races, giving him 27 victories in the 1967 season. That is more single-season wins than any NASCAR driver before him—or since.

■ ■ ■

Growing up in tiny Level Cross, North Carolina, Richard always knew he wanted to be a race-car driver. His father, Lee, was a NASCAR champion and the winner of the very first Daytona 500.

Cars and racing were Petty family passions—Richard and his mother and brother would follow Lee from race to race. Richard's brother found success as an engine builder and mechanic. Richard followed his father onto the tracks.

In 1959, one year after he started racing, Richard was named NASCAR's Rookie of the

Richard and his father, Lee, in 1960.

Year. That year he also raced in the very first Daytona 500 ever run. Five years later, he won the Daytona 500—and would go on to win that race six more times in his career. He would also become the first driver to win seven NASCAR championship cups. Only one other driver in NASCAR history, Dale Earnhardt, Sr., has won that many championships.

In his thirty-five-year career, Richard won 200 races—almost double the number of any other driver ever to race in NASCAR. Richard was so successful that everyone calls him the King.

Richard has always been known as one of NASCAR's friendliest drivers. He stops to chat and sign autographs—sometimes hundreds of them a day—for his fans. He won NASCAR's Most Popular Driver award nine times. Many people think of Richard as the unofficial spokesperson of NASCAR.

Richard and his 1957 Oldsmobile convertible at the first annual Daytona 500 in 1959. He fell out of the race because of engine failure.

One of Richard's fans was himself a very famous man—Ronald Reagan, the president of the United States from 1981 to 1989. When Richard won the 200th race of his career, President Reagan met him on the track to congratulate him.

With President Ronald Reagan on July 4, 1984.

In 1992, another president honored Richard's accomplishments. President George H. W. Bush gave Richard the Presidential Medal of Freedom. This is the highest award given in the United States to a nonmilitary person. It's presented to people who have reached the top of their field. Richard was the first motor sports athlete ever awarded this important medal.

President George H. W. Bush presents the Medal of Freedom to Richard in the White House.

Though Richard retired in 1992, he's still very active in NASCAR. He's the head of Petty Racing, which owns two NASCAR teams. One of those teams has a driver who is extra special to Richard—his son, Kyle Petty.

Almost always seen in his trademark sunglasses and cowboy hat, Richard is one of NASCAR's all-time greatest stars. His famous #43 car is even in the collection of the Smithsonian National Museum of American History in Washington, D.C.

Richard and his #43 car at the Smithsonian Institution.

Richard Petty

(b. 1937)

- Won 200 races, almost twice as many as any other driver in NASCAR history
- Won seven NASCAR championships (tied with Dale Earnhardt, Sr.)
- Seven-time winner of Daytona 500
- Record number of wins in one season— twenty-seven in 1967
- Over 700 top-ten finishes in 1,185 starts
- Earned the most pole positions in NASCAR history
- Started the most races in NASCAR history
- International Motorsports Hall of Fame
- Motorsports Hall of Fame in America
- Named one of NASCAR's 50 Greatest Drivers
- Nine-time NASCAR Most Popular Driver
- Rookie of the Year, 1959
- Presidential Medal of Freedom

Dale Earnhardt, Sr.

(1951–2001)

February 15, 1998. Daytona Beach, Florida. The famous Daytona 500 has begun. It's the first—and most important—race of the entire season. Winning this race is like winning the Super Bowl in football or the World Series in baseball.

Dale Earnhardt is one of the top drivers in the race. He's one of the very best NASCAR drivers in history. But after 19 tries, he's never won the Daytona 500.

It is lap number 199 out of 200. Dale is in the lead. The fans are on their feet, screaming and cheering. Several cars trail just seconds behind Dale's black #3 Chevy. Dale presses the gas pedal to the floor and flies through the lap. One last time around the track and Dale sees the famous black-and-white-checkered flags that signal the end of each race. He sails through them. The crowd goes wild! Dale has finally "got the checkered" and won the Daytona 500!

He drives his car to Victory Lane to wait for his trophy. Members of every team line up to congratulate him. Even Dale's biggest rivals are there. No one has ever seen this happen before.

■ ■ ■

Dale celebrates winning the Daytona 500, February 15, 1998.

Dale's father, Ralph, was a race-car driver who taught him all about racing. He taught Dale to work hard and never give up. Dale's father was tough on him, but he just wanted his son to do his best—in racing and in life.

When Dale was a teenager, he began to race cars around his hometown of Kannapolis, North Carolina. Dale loved racing so much, he dropped out of high school. He wanted to spend all his time getting better at racing. Dale's father was very sad that his son did not graduate. Dale later said he wished he had stayed in school.

In 1979, Dale got his big break. A man named Rod Osterlund asked Dale to drive one of his cars on the NASCAR circuit. That year, he was named NASCAR Rookie of the Year.

The next season, Dale did something no one had ever done before. He won the NASCAR championship cup in only his second year of racing! He would win an amazing *seven* championship cups in his career. Only one other driver, Richard Petty, has won that many.

Dale stands in Victory Lane after his first Winston Cup win on April 1, 1979.

Even though Dale was respected for his many victories, he was not always liked by other drivers or racing fans. He was called the Intimidator because he would do whatever it took to win a race—even bump into other drivers' cars to get them out of the way during a competition. He once said, "Bumpers were made for bumping!" Some thought he was a bully on the track. But no one could deny he was a great driver.

Sadly, Dale was killed while racing the Daytona 500. It was February 18, 2001, on the final turn of the last lap. The race was just seconds from being over. Dale's car and another car bumped, throwing Dale's #3 into a wall at 180 miles per hour. The Intimidator died instantly. The racing world was stunned. Dale's fans call that day Black Sunday. Newspapers all over the country ran front-page stories about the crash.

Even today, years after his death, fans continue to buy keepsakes with his name and car number. Dale Earnhardt, Sr., will always be remembered as a NASCAR legend.

Following Dale's death, fans created a memorial in front of Dale Earnhardt Inc. headquarters.

Dale Earnhardt, Sr.

(1951–2001)

- Won seven NASCAR championships (tied for the most with Richard Petty)
- Won 1998 Daytona 500
- 76 wins, 428 top-ten finishes
- Rookie of the Year, 1979
- Only driver to win back-to-back Rookie of the Year (1979) and NASCAR championship cup (1980)
- First on all-time-winnings list, with more than $40 million won
- 2001 NASCAR Most Popular Driver
- One of NASCAR's 50 Greatest Drivers
- International Motorsports Hall of Fame
- Motorsports Hall of Fame in America

Jeff Gordon

(b. 1971)

August 6, 1994. Indianapolis, Indiana. Jeff
Gordon has just celebrated his twenty-third
birthday. Now he's ready to drive in an event
that will change the history of racing. Never
before has a NASCAR race been held at the
Indianapolis Motor Speedway, Indiana's most
famous racetrack. Since 1916, only the great
Indy 500 has been held here. Soon the brand-new
Brickyard 400 will become one of NASCAR's
most important races.

Jeff trailing Ernie
Irvan at the
Brickyard 400,
August 6, 1994.

Some Indy fans are angry that NASCAR has come to their track. They don't want a NASCAR race to be held at Indy's most famous spot. Still, the race is sold out.

Just one year before, Jeff was named the 1993 NASCAR Rookie of the Year. Today is a chance to prove that he is on his way to being one of NASCAR's best.

It is nearly three hours into the race. With only five laps to go, Ernie Irvan is in the lead. Jeff, in second place, tries hard to catch him. Suddenly the crowd is shocked to see Ernie slow down. His right front tire has gone flat! Ernie leaves the track and heads to the pit to get it fixed. Jeff holds tight to his lead and soon roars across the finish line! He's won today's landmark race. Jeff has proven himself as one of NASCAR's next great superstars.

■ ■ ■

Jeff always loved racing. He started competing in quarter midget cars when he was just five

Jeff in Victory Lane after winning the first Brickyard 400 event.

years old! In 1977, Simpson Racing Products
made its smallest racing suit ever for six-year-old
Jeff. He later moved on to racing go-karts and
sprint cars.

When Jeff was thirteen years old, his family
moved from California to Indiana so he could
compete in a state known for sprint-car racing.
After several years, Jeff realized there would be
more chances to compete if he changed to stock-
car racing. His NASCAR career was born.

Jeff's first NASCAR race was a turning point
not just for him but for the sport itself. That race
at the Atlanta Motor Speedway was the very last
one run by Richard Petty, the King of NASCAR.
Some look back on it as the moment when the
NASCAR crown was handed over to Jeff. He
would soon come to be known as the Kid and the
Wonder Boy. In 1995—just three years later—Jeff
jumped into the history books. He became the
youngest NASCAR champion since 1950. And
Jeff's best year ever was soon to come.

Thirteen-year-old sprint-car racer Jeff Gordon.

In 1998, Jeff won thirteen races in thirty-three tries. Only Richard Petty has ever won that many races in one season! He also finished twenty-eight times in the top ten and twenty-six times in the top five. He had a four-race winning streak, which tied a record. And he won more than $9.3 million. Richard Petty didn't win that much in his entire career! Jeff topped the year off by winning his third NASCAR championship. Jeff and his #24 car could not be beaten.

By the year 2000, Jeff had won fifty races. Just ten other drivers in NASCAR history have

Car #24 crosses yet another finish line in 1998.

In New York's Times Square on December 4, 1998, Jeff celebrates his third Winston Cup.

matched this feat. He is also a four-time NASCAR champion. Only two drivers, Richard Petty and Dale Earnhardt, Sr., have won more championships.

Jeff is a very popular driver, and not only with racing fans. Several companies have hired him to promote their products. He's hosted television shows and appeared in movies. You can even buy a Jeff Gordon action figure!

Many people see Jeff as the face of today's

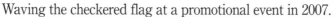

Waving the checkered flag at a promotional event in 2007.

NASCAR. They believe he's the driver who has made NASCAR so popular. He's polite and well spoken. He always makes time to talk to news crews and fans. He often says he owes his success to his pit crew, who are called the Rainbow Warriors because Jeff's car is so colorful.

Jeff still has many years of racing ahead of him. With all the success he's had so far, it will be exciting to see what he achieves in the future!

The Rainbow Warriors at work on Jeff's #24 car.

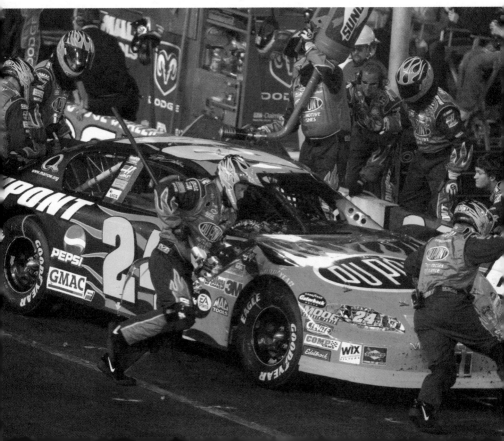

Jeff Gordon

(b. 1971)

- Has won four NASCAR championships
- In 2001, earned most winnings in a single season (over $10 million)
- Youngest champion in NASCAR's modern era
- Rookie of the Year, 1993
- Has won seventy-nine races (so far)
- Has finished in top ten every year since 1994
- Has won three Daytona 500s
- Sixth on all-time-wins list
- 1997 Winston Million winner
- One of NASCAR's 50 Greatest Drivers

More NASCAR Greats

The men you have just read about are four of the top NASCAR drivers of all time. But there are many more men *and* women who have been outstanding NASCAR racers. Here are a few of them.

Sara Christian (1918–1980) competed in 1949 in NASCAR's very first race, held in Charlotte, North Carolina. She didn't win that day, but she made history as the first woman to drive in a NASCAR race. Later that year, Sara finished once in the top five and twice in the top ten. No other woman has matched her NASCAR record! She was named Woman Driver of the Year by the United States Drivers Association in 1949. Sara also made history when she and her husband, Frank, became the only husband and wife in NASCAR history to compete in the same race. Sara raced for only two years, but she's regarded as one of the legends of NASCAR.

Sara in Charlotte, North Carolina, June 19, 1949.

Bill Elliott (b. 1955) came to be known as Million-Dollar Bill in 1985. That year, the R. J. Reynolds company promised a $1 million bonus to any driver who could win three of the Big Four NASCAR races: the Daytona 500, Talladega's Winston 500, Charlotte's World 600, and Darlington's Southern 500. Bill won at Daytona and Talladega but lost in Charlotte. Reporters and fans packed the stands at

Darlington to watch Bill's last chance to win the million. Bill zoomed through the checkered flags only six-tenths of a *second* ahead. In that fraction of a second, he won the biggest one-day paycheck in NASCAR history. Just two years later, he proved to be the fastest NASCAR driver ever when he ran a lap at an incredible 212.809 miles per hour! A truly nice guy, Bill was named Most Popular Driver a record sixteen times.

Bill wins $1 million at Darlington in the Southern 500, September 1, 1985.

Janet Guthrie (b. 1938) started flying airplanes at age seventeen. After getting a physics degree and training with NASA, Janet began flying around racetracks. In 1977, she became the first woman driver to compete in the Daytona 500. She didn't win, but she was named Top Rookie in that race and in five others that year. Janet also drove Indy cars and was the first woman ever to drive in the Indianapolis 500. She was voted into the International Women's Sports Hall of Fame and the International Motorsports Hall of Fame. Today, Janet's racing helmet and suit are in the collection of the Smithsonian National Museum of American History in Washington, D.C.

David Pearson (b. 1934) was an outstanding NASCAR driver. Just ask the great Richard Petty, who says David was the best driver in NASCAR history. David won three NASCAR championships. He also won 105 races

Janet puts on fire-resistant gloves before heading out on the Daytona International Speedway course, July 2, 1976.

in his career. That number puts him second on the all-time-wins list! David was called the Silver Fox by other drivers because of his sly, sneaky style on the racetrack. He had a way of pulling tricks that made him seem to come out of nowhere to pass other drivers and win! Always cool and confident in his actions and his driving, David lives up to Richard Petty's words.

David Pearson after winning the Daytona International Speedway's Firecracker 400, July 4, 1974.